HEART OF
EPHESIANS

DEVOTIONAL

Copyright © 2016 CF Church

All rights reserved.

ISBN: 1530452759
ISBN-13: 978-1530452750

Available from Amazon.com, Kindle and other retail outlets.

ABOUT THE AUTHOR

A pastor at Christian Fellowship Church since 1990, Kent is married to Pam, and they have three married children and seven grandchildren. As Senior Pastor, his passion is to help people grow into their unique place of ministry in the Body of Christ. In addition to carrying the vision God has for Christian Fellowship, Kent is focused on preaching, teaching and leadership development.

PREFACE

Before you begin using this devotional, I want you to know my intention and purpose in writing. It is my passion that you would learn to open God's Word and hear Him speak personally to your spirit. God is very much alive, and He desires to speak to us regularly through His Word.

What has been written is what I heard God speak to me. It may or may not be the words He would speak to you, but there is something He is speaking through each passage in Ephesians. So what is contained here is a personal word that God might say to you. It is intentionally in the first person to illustrate that very fact.

In writing this, there were many times when I felt a unique touch of the Lord. It is, therefore, my belief that some of what was written is from the Lord for you.

Here is how I suggest you proceed: start by praying and asking the Holy Spirit to speak to you; then read the passage, and quietly meditate on what it says, listening to what God might speak to you; after that, if you desire or if it feels like you need help in hearing, read what is written and, perhaps, the Lord will enlighten you to a fresh aspect of the passage. The purpose is twofold: first, to grow in and encounter more deeply the love of Jesus; second, to continue developing an ear to hear His voice speak personally.

There are a few people I would like to thank before you begin reading. Thanks to: Kathy Carr, who spent hours with a careful eye proofing this material; Matt

Sommerfield, who, being blessed with creativity, took the concept, put a picture around what God was speaking and prepared it for publishing; Aaron Searles, who lent another set of eyes to look through the content and consider the doctrine of what was written.

Love and appreciation goes to my wife, Pam, who supports and encourages me, in every way, to pursue God and answer His call. Last but not least, I am grateful to you, the reader, and blessed that you would take the time for this devotional. I pray fervently that we would all be touched and moved by the Holy Spirit as we experience Ephesians together.

In His Grace,

KENT ATKINSON
Senior Pastor
Christian Fellowship Church

DAY ONE

Paul, an apostle of Christ Jesus by the will of God, To God's holy people in Ephesus, the faithful in Christ Jesus: Grace and peace to you from God our Father and the Lord Jesus Christ.
– Ephesians 1:1-2 NIV

My will has intentional purposes for Your life. The course I have for Your life, along with the influence you are to have, is found in My will. It cannot be earned, manipulated or presumed.

My will for Paul was apostleship, and it was made clear to him. So it is that My will for your life is being made clear to you. Paul chose to accept My will for him and walk fully in it. The influence he had was from Me, enabled by living in My will.

Will you choose to accept what I have for you? Once you surrender to My will, you can rest in the knowledge that the influence you need will come from Me, and I hold the outcome in My hand.

DAY TWO

Praise be to the God and Father of our Lord Jesus Christ, who has blessed us in the heavenly realms with every spiritual blessing in Christ.
– Ephesians 1:3 NIV

The heavenly realm is not as far away as you think. Just the opposite: this realm is closer than your breath. Heaven is the realm of My Spirit, which I have placed inside you. In this realm is every spiritual resource you need…not "someday," but today!

What blessing or resource are you in need of? Is it salvation, grace, inner strength or simply a fresh deposit of My love? Through faith-filled prayer, pull it out of heaven and onto earth. These blessings are not available on earth except to those who humbly ask heaven to invade their world. What do you need today? It is yours!

DAY THREE

For he chose us in him before the creation of the world to be holy and blameless in his sight.
– Ephesians 1:4 NIV

Never forget that I chose you! Long before your parents met, I desired relationship with you. My choice is not dependent on anything but My will. Not on your heritage, personality, talent, choices made or anything you have done or have yet to do.

Provision is made for the spiritually-genetic stain of sin that marked you. Now you can voluntarily choose to respond to My pursuit of you. Through My sacrifice, I see you as righteous now. The stain on your soul has been cleansed, opening up the opportunity for intimate relationship. Remember that how you feel about yourself has no bearing on how I feel about you. I chose you and love you deeply.

DAY FOUR

In love he predestined us for adoption to sonship through Jesus Christ, in accordance with his pleasure and will—
– Ephesians 1:5 NIV

Dear child...for that is what you are: My child, part of My family. This was My will from the start. Your adoption was not a "sterile" contract. No, it flowed out of My heart of love and filled Me with pleasure to adopt you.

Be sure of this: I have been planning your place in My family since the beginning of time, patiently waiting for your acceptance of My offer. There is so much I want to show you about what it means to be part of My family. Ask Me what this means for you today.

Rest securely in the fact that nothing can separate us. It excites Me to think of all I have planned for you!

DAY FIVE

In love he predestined us for adoption to sonship through Jesus Christ, in accordance with his pleasure and will—to the praise of his glorious grace, which he has freely given us in the One he loves.
– Ephesians 1:5-6 NIV

My grace is being freely poured out through My One and Only Beloved Son. It is provided for you and brings Me praise. Open your hands to receive this gift, for this will make My praise glorious. This means letting go of every notion of self-attainment or self-promotion. Let go of every impulse to prove or qualify yourself. You cannot receive My deluge of grace while holding these things.

Do you desire to see My praise multiplied in your life? Let go of these proud and petty remnants of who you were, and receive My grace that is transforming you into who I created you to be. What do you need to let go of today?

DAY SIX

In him we have redemption through his blood, the forgiveness of sins, in accordance with the riches of God's grace that he lavished on us. With all wisdom and understanding,
– *Ephesians 1:7-8 NIV*

My redemption restores everything that was lost through sin. When I forgive, it is not simply absolution, it is reinstatement. The blood of My Son has cleansed you and opened the treasure of grace that restores the significance of who you are which sin had stolen.

No longer paralyzed by shame, you are free to live out the redemptive purposes that are in My heart for you. My grace and redemption go hand-in-hand to bring about the unmerited favor that restores innocence. Now I see you as blameless and holy.

Sweet child, can you see yourself through My eyes? What change of perspective does this bring?

DAY SEVEN

With all wisdom and understanding, he made known to us the mystery of his will according to his good pleasure, which he purposed in Christ, to be put into effect when the times reach their fulfillment—to bring unity to all things in heaven and on earth under Christ.

– Ephesians 1:8-10 NIV

The mystery of My will is now revealed. I have purposed to bridge the chasm between things of heaven (eternal) and things of earth (temporal) through My Son, Jesus. Your faith and hope in Him break the barriers that separate these realms. In My Son, I have reunited you with My eternal love.

How I have longed for this time when the decaying effects of sin would be reversed in you. No longer does fear hold dominance over you, for there is no fear in My eternal love. Disillusionment and despair are rooted in the temporal and find no place in the realm of heaven. Though these things may feel real on earth, they are the antithesis of My realm.

Trust in Me; hope in My Son, and remember that I have placed eternity in you. Begin to see things in light of that; see things as I see them. What are the places in you or circumstances around you where I can unite My heaven with your earth?

DAY EIGHT

In him we were also chosen, having been predestined according to the plan of him who works out everything in conformity with the purpose of his will, in order that we, who were the first to put our hope in Christ, might be for the praise of his glory.
– Ephesians 1:11-12 NIV

Beloved, I see the plans of your heart. That which captures your mind and occupies your heart is not hidden from Me. I have a plan for your life and have intimate knowledge of what will satisfy and give full expression to who you are.

From the very beginning, I have been working to see My heart for you expressed in the experiences of your life. This can only be obstructed by the choices you make in pursuing or rejecting My plans. Rejection of My plans is not always in the form of obstinate rebellion, though that certainly works to obstruct. Passivity has an equal power in moving you off the course I have for you.

Know this, nothing and no one has the power to stop Me from bringing all in your life into conformity with My will—My good, pleasing and perfect will. Are there areas of passivity that have stymied My plans for you? How can your experiences come more into line with My will for you?

DAY NINE

And you also were included in Christ when you heard the message of truth, the gospel of your salvation. When you believed, you were marked in him with a seal, the promised Holy Spirit, who is a deposit guaranteeing our inheritance until the redemption of those who are God's possession—to the praise of his glory.

– Ephesians 1:13-14 NIV

There is so much confusion about the Holy Spirit and My work through Him in your life. Don't you know He is the promise you received at your salvation? Your spirit made alive in My Spirit, permanently altering the course of your life. As important as this is, there is so much more found in Him!

The Holy Spirit resides in you, securing all that has been given to you as My child. Inheritance was passed along to My heirs through the death of My Son. The Holy Spirit is the executor of My estate. All you have need of, My Spirit provides out of My unending supply...power over darkness, insight and revelation, peace beyond human understanding, and joy that flows from heaven. All of this and more is yours by My design and My Holy Spirit's presence in you.

Practice, this day, the constant awareness of the Holy Spirit's companionship. Ask and He will give generously of the resources found in Me.

DAY TEN

For this reason, ever since I heard about your faith in the Lord Jesus and your love for all God's people, I have not stopped giving thanks for you, remembering you in my prayers.
– Ephesians 1:15-16 NIV

Dear one, in whom I delight, do you know how many in your life have sought My face in regard to you? Prayer for you has come from many saints in so many places, both known and unknown to you. They have joined in intercession with My Son, Jesus. The effect of those prayers is immeasurable for you. My favor, My protection, My direction and My sovereign guidance have been the result of those who sought Me on your behalf.

It is so important that you know this: you are not alone in this walk on earth. There are many who walk beside you in love and faithfulness. And My presence is with you always. My Son is praying for things that you need and are not presently aware of. As the comfort and encouragement rises in you, do not forget that, today, I am using you to pray for those in your life, that the great and grand purposes I have for them would be realized.

DAY ELEVEN

I keep asking that the God of our Lord Jesus Christ, the glorious Father, may give you the Spirit of wisdom and revelation, so that you may know him better.
– Ephesians 1:17 NIV

Your desire to know Me brings delight to Me. Wisdom and revelation are available by My Spirit so that you may come into a more intimate knowledge of Me. This cannot be accomplished through your mind or your human understanding. Therefore, open up to My Spirit, and I will reveal Myself to you. My secrets are made available so you may know what's on My heart. I will show you what I desire, and I will show you what I am doing.

To know Me is to experience Me at a deeper and more profound level than ever before. I desire to give you experiences in the Spirit that will open up to you the depths of who I am. I am unending love, I am overflowing joy, I am faithful, I am good and I am just. All the depths of wisdom and knowledge are found in Me; no one can know them except as I reveal them. Therefore, discipline yourself and quiet your mind from the noise of earth. Seek to activate your spirit so I may give revelation of all that is true about Me.

DAY TWELVE

I pray that the eyes of your heart may be enlightened in order that you may know the hope to which he has called you, the riches of his glorious inheritance in his holy people,
– Ephesians 1:18 NIV

Today I desire to highlight and reveal the great hope that I have placed within you. That is, the hope of glory found in My Son, Jesus, which anchors against all that would assail you. This hope is the certainty of what you do not see with your eyes but you know has been given you in the Spirit.

I withhold nothing from you, but you must learn to see with the eyes of the Spirit what is already yours. This hope revealed is life to you and relieves the great burden you have picked up while walking through the darkness of the earthly realm.

What do you carry that is from fear, worry, or need to control the future? This hope of glory and delight of heaven is yours for today. What troubles you, dear one, and darkens your horizon? I am here now to open your eyes to the hope that is in Me. All My promises are 'yes' in Christ.

DAY THIRTEEN

...and his incomparably great power for us who believe.
– Ephesians 1:19 NIV

You are the one I love; you are the apple of My eye; the center of My focus is on you. There is nothing and no one on earth that can separate you from this great love and affection that I have for you. Out of this love, I have given you My power by placing the Holy Spirit within you. This power flows out of the realm of the Spirit, fulfilling the work that I am doing inside of you.

Regardless of what is taking place outside of and all around you, please know that My power is mightily working with you to accomplish the things I desire for you. These things have very little to do with your role or your status or your circumstance. They have everything to do with your identity and your purpose, born in Me before you came into being. As you come to understand this and appropriate the power that I have given you, it will begin to flow out and alter the circumstances of your life.

I have promised to bring heaven to earth through you. Before this can take place, you must learn about the power I have given you in the realm of heaven. When the things of earth press in and cause you to feel powerless, center yourself on the power that I have given you within, for nothing can diminish that power. It will provide everything that you need to walk through the circumstances of your life.

DAY FOURTEEN

…and his incomparably great power for us who believe. That power is the same as the mighty strength he exerted when he raised Christ from the dead and seated him at his right hand in the heavenly realms,
– Ephesians 1:19-20 NIV

Beloved, I see all that is inside of you, both the places that are alive with My presence and the areas that have died from lack of hope, death-evoking effects of sin or the shriveling words of others. I have placed My Spirit in you, and He has the power to make all things new.

I bring life to every place that is under the curse of death. My Spirit, which I have placed inside of you, will resurrect everything that has been smothered by the effects of death. Surrender every barren place, every lifeless area inside of you to the power that I have placed there.

This power that raised My Son from the dead is made available to you. Believe that it will also give life to the dead places that exist inside if you. These are not to be raised to what they were but, rather, be made new in every way. This is My plan as you come fully into the new creation that I have made you to be.

DAY FIFTEEN

...and his incomparably great power for us who believe. That power is the same as the mighty strength he exerted when he raised Christ from the dead and seated him at his right hand in the heavenly realms,
– *Ephesians 1:19-20 NIV*

Oh, how I long for you to understand the dimensions of the power that I have given you. The way to access this resource is counterintuitive for you. Instead of striving to "power up" in your flesh or in your own creativity and ingenuity, realize this resource requires just the opposite. My power is freely available when you open yourself to it through submission and surrender to the work I am doing inside of you.

My Son is with Me in heaven, and the Holy Spirit has been given on earth to ensure that the resources stored in heaven can be made available to you. Cease striving to accomplish great things or reach for pressing goals. My strength becomes manifest when you embrace the knowledge of your weakness. Simply rest in that knowledge, and walk in the center of My will. My power is made available for you to reach the destiny I have placed in your heart.

DAY SIXTEEN

...far above all rule and authority, power and dominion, and every name that is invoked, not only in the present age but also in the one to come.
– Ephesians 1:21 NIV

Dear child, it gives me pain to see you living in so much fear. When things occur in your life that seem so very much out of control, it fills you with dread for the future. Hear this, and let it mark your soul: My Son has full dominion over everything that exists in heaven and on earth. All authority is His; therefore, no one and nothing can harm you when you live under My authority.

Hide yourself in the shelter of My wings; know that I am your protector and that I watch over your life, both your coming and your going. The arms of My all-encompassing authority surround you with safety and comfort. You are prone to cry, too, when you are in distress. Cry out to Me, invoke the name of My Son, Jesus, and all dominion and rule that I possess will be yours. For I have placed all things under Him so nothing you face is outside of His control.

DAY SEVENTEEN

And God placed all things under his feet and appointed him to be head over everything for the church, which is his body, the fullness of him who fills everything in every way.
– Ephesians 1:22-23 NIV

My Spirit has been given so that, through believers everywhere, My presence could fill every place on earth. More than that—much more than that—is the role of My Spirit to fill in you everything in every way. My Spirit, the Spirit of Jesus, stands at the entrance to the areas of your life that have been closed off to Me. I knock and do not assert entry until invited. Will you open these closed areas that are remnants of the fear and darkness in which you lived before My Spirit came inside of you?

It is My desire to fill you full in every way, but I will not force entry to the areas where you desire to retain control. It is in these areas where pain and suffering continue to poison your life. I desire to bring the full expression of My Presence into these areas so that you can be made whole. Wholeness is only accomplished when My Spirit fills everything in every way.

DAY EIGHTEEN

As for you, you were dead in your transgressions and sins...
– Ephesians 2:1 NIV

Before you encountered My grace, the deeds that filled your life flowed out of the darkness which engulfed your spirit. You once were dead in sin, and the natural behavior flowing out of that death further sealed the desperate condition you lived in.

All that has changed, now that I have resurrected your spirit by the power that raised My Son from the grave. Though your behavior, attitudes and motives are not perfect and pure, they need no longer feed a cycle of death, for My grace covers you. Since you have tasted the light of My life after having been in the despair of darkness, stand firm against the assault of the enemy's temptation and deception. Live this day out of what you know is true: you have been covered by My grace, I have redeemed your life from the pit of despair, and I have filled you with strength to stand your ground against temptation that leads to transgression.

DAY NINETEEN

As for you, you were dead in your transgressions and sins, in which you used to live when you followed the ways of this world and of the ruler of the kingdom of the air, the spirit who is now at work in those who are disobedient.
– *Ephesians 2:1-2 NIV*

My dear child, do not let your past reach out and control your life now and in the future. There was a time when you were caught up in a world distorted and warped by the adversary. His kingdom is a kingdom of darkness, but I have called you out of darkness into light. So you must forget your shame, shake off the blame and step into the newness of the life I'm giving you from this day forward.

There was a time when the core of your heart was disobedient, hostile and rebellious toward Me. But My love has broken through all that—it is now a thing of the past. Now your heart has turned toward Me, and I have made My residence at the core of your being, your spirit. So I say forget what is behind and press on to the future I have for you. Press on to the new purposes that I have for you to glorify Me in.

Though I have given the ruler of the kingdom of the air dominion over those who are disobedient, this is no longer true for you. Under My rule and My dominion, the adversary has no hold on you. Do not listen to the lie that your past can bar you from the good things I have for you in the future. Sever that past, and move into My kingdom of light.

DAY TWENTY

All of us also lived among them at one time, gratifying the cravings of our flesh and following its desires and thoughts. Like the rest, we were by nature deserving of wrath.
– Ephesians 2:3 NIV

You cannot know the depth of My grace unless you've lived under the fear of My wrath. I am a God of justice; My character requires that injustice, oppression and transgression be remedied. My wrath, therefore, is an extension of My justice, and justice an expression of My love. This love of justice is equal to My love for you. Therefore, rejoice beloved, for the requirements of My justice have been met in My Son, your Savior, Jesus Christ.

Though at one time you were an object of My wrath, you have always been an object of My love. Your willingness to accept My grace has satisfied justice and brings you fully around into the circle of love. I love you so deeply that I am compelled to rescue you. Let My kindness lead you through repentance and into My embrace. Never again are you vulnerable to wrath, for now you are eternally secured by My grace. Lift up your countenance, and take joy in your redemption today.

DAY TWENTY-ONE

But because of his great love for us, God, who is rich in mercy, made us alive with Christ even when we were dead in transgressions—it is by grace you have been saved.
– Ephesians 2:4-5 NIV

I have placed the capacity in you for My life to be experienced. This is the very same life My Son was filled with while on earth. Eternal life is not just for the "after death" eternity, but for "in the present" eternity as it flows from Me and runs through your heart. Learn what it means to lay hold of life that is true life.

Human existence without the breath of My Spirit is a sham, filled with fleeting pleasures, discontentment and pain. You crave life that has substance, that endures, that makes sense...and rightly so. When My Spirit abides in you and awakens you, My glory rests on you, and My life, which is permanent, anchors you. The sham of life apart from Me is shown for what it is.

I have made you alive in My Son! Live out of that life, and the issues that loom large on earth shrink to nothing in light of the eternal life we are sharing together. What issue are you facing that I can give proper perspective on? Cast your cares on Me, and I will ease your burden. Give it to Me today, and think no more of it—let it drop.

DAY TWENTY-TWO

And God raised us up with Christ and seated us with him in the heavenly realms in Christ Jesus, in order that in the coming ages he might show the incomparable riches of his grace, expressed in his kindness to us in Christ Jesus.
– Ephesians 2:6-7 NIV

My authority has been given; I have given you the keys to the kingdom in order to bring the reign of heaven into your earthly existence. The authority I give you is neither exercised in nor accessed through earth's realm. My authority is given by spending time in the realm of the Spirit.

I say this so you may understand more fully—not only do I come into your world, but I have given you a seat with My Son in heaven. You have a place in heaven given to you by My grace. You must learn to dwell in this place, for it is there you learn the ways of My kingdom; it is there you learn the way of My authority; it is there that you gain perspective and insight into what I am doing; it is there that you are strengthened in your body to do My will.

So right now, in this moment, leave the distractions of this world, and come spend time with Me in the heavenlies. Whatever needs that manifest in your life this day will be supplied.

DAY TWENTY-THREE

For it is by grace you have been saved, through faith—and this is not from yourselves, it is the gift of God— not by works, so that no one can boast.
– Ephesians 2:8-9 NIV

Strengthen the muscle of faith that brought the gift of salvation to you and, even now, secures you in grace. Confront anything that would seek to diminish the value of My grace. Confront the compulsion to earn or qualify for My favor.

Through My creative order, the grace I give is, by nature, unearned favor requiring no qualifications. Your adversary always attacks My creative work. The full freedom I have for you is found in complete, untainted acceptance of My grace. The gift is free, but unfettered acceptance costs you something—pride, independence and need of self-accomplishment must go.

The key to My life is found in the surrender of spiritual achievement and the release of your striving. This is found in a constant consciousness of your dependence on My grace. Gird up your faith, and trust in My promise to pour over you My unquenchable grace.

DAY TWENTY-FOUR

For we are God's handiwork, created in Christ Jesus to do good works, which God prepared in advance for us to do.
— *Ephesians 2:10 NIV*

The desire you have to live a life filled with purpose, significance and the substance of things that matter was knit into your being by Me at creation, then reawakened at salvation, that you might be an instrument of My glory on earth. A pathway has already been established and laid down for you to walk in and fulfill this design for purpose in your life.

The things that make you unique and different are not random acts but are designed intentions by Me, your Creator, for the significant work your life will be. Make no mistake, this work has no bearing on My favor and love for you, but it opens up in you places of satisfaction and joy that would otherwise be unreachable.

My child, follow what you know to be My will, and do not be afraid, for I have gone before you, in advance, to prepare the way for your success. What are the steps for you to take today? Cast off timidity, and in bold confidence, move into the good works I have prepared for this day.

DAY TWENTY-FIVE

Therefore, remember that formerly you who are Gentiles by birth and called "uncircumcised" by those who call themselves "the circumcision" (which is done in the body by human hands)— remember that at that time you were separate from Christ, excluded from citizenship in Israel and foreigners to the covenants of the promise, without hope and without God in the world. But now in Christ Jesus you who once were far away have been brought near by the blood of Christ.
– Ephesians 2:11-13 NIV

Every promise in My Word I have assigned to you. You have heard about My chosen race, Israel, and how I set them apart and chose them to reveal My glory on earth. Now I say you are My chosen one, in whom I take great delight. In you and through you, I will reveal My glory to this world. Once your name was "outcast" and "foreigner," but now I call you "beloved child," "friend" and "bride."

Here are My promises to you: I have brought you near, I will be intimate with you and reveal My secrets; nothing can separate you from My love, absolutely nothing; in Me you are a conqueror; there is no circumstance that I cannot work in your life for good; My grace will always be sufficient for you; in your weakness, I will be made strong. Dear one, be filled with faith, for every promise I have made to you will be fulfilled. Which of the many promises I have spoken will you hold onto today in the midst of what you face?

DAY TWENTY-SIX

For he himself is our peace, who has made the two groups one and has destroyed the barrier, the dividing wall of hostility,
– Ephesians 2:14 NIV

Why does My peace allude you this day? It is flowing like a river in your life, and yet you stand so far from the shores. Your mind and heart have wandered off into places that disturb you and make you feel that you have lost control. You wander off in confusion because you do not understand true peace.

My peace is not just the removal of hostility or the absence of tension, but it is the alignment of righteousness, the infusion of wholeness and well-being. Come to Me and find peace, and understand what that peace may bring. When I bring peace, there is a choppy transition from chaos to order. When you call on Me for peace, tensions may rise as I bring righteousness to infuse the situation that you face. Rest assured that no matter what the circumstance looks like, My peace will prevail and bring things into order, causing a sense of well-being in every situation that you give to Me.

Meanwhile, look to Me and have your heart put at ease in My presence. Drink deeply from My river of peace so that, in the midst of transition, there can be a calm that goes beyond human understanding. Where do you need to become an agent of My peace today in your world? Come to Me so I can reassure you that I am in control, and I will bring order out of the chaos surrounding your life.

DAY TWENTY-SEVEN

For he himself is our peace, who has made the two groups one and has destroyed the barrier, the dividing wall of hostility, by setting aside in his flesh the law with its commands and regulations. His purpose was to create in himself one new humanity out of the two, thus making peace,
– Ephesians 2:14-15 NIV

There are relationships in your life that are still characterized by hostility, relationships where the need to be right supersedes My call to live in peace. I have not called you to live in sin in order to be in unity; rather, there is a new law at work and that is the law of love.

I have broken down the barriers that separate people from one another. It is time to release the hostility you feel and open your heart to the freedom that comes when you forgive. The unity I give is supernatural; therefore, it begins at the invisible level, inside of you. It will eventually bear fruit in your natural, visible world, but it begins in the unseen places.

There are untenable relationships that, on a human level, make unity seem impossible. I tell you, in Me all reconciliation is possible. My love is extended to those you find so difficult to live in harmony with. In your actions, you deny the extent of My love. Those are ones I have reached out to just as much as I have reached out to you. Allow Me to put the same love I have for them in your heart, and you will find peace, freedom and release.

DAY TWENTY-EIGHT

and in one body to reconcile both of them to God through the cross, by which he put to death their hostility.
– Ephesians 2:16 NIV

Humankind gathers at the foot of the cross with a desperate need for a Savior. There is only one approach to the cross—that is, through humility. The same attitude that led My Son to the cross to die and shed His blood is what leads you to come. The cross is for you and your need to be restored in relationship with Me. Come to the cross, first with the transgression you walked in and with repentance for what you've done, then with the pain you have caused others.

It is in this place, at the foot of the cross, you begin to gain perspective on the brokenness that resides in all humankind. It is what drives the behavior and the attitudes of others who have hurt you. Let your heart be moved with understanding, tenderness and love, just like mine, for those who are trapped in the pain that oozes from their own brokenness.

How can you hold judgment and hostility toward those who are driven by the same "hole in the soul" in which you once lived? Your heart weighs sin from bad to worse, but that is not how I deem it. All sin is equally egregious from start to finish. Let the grace flowing in My blood that pours from the cross heal your pain and forgive you. Relationship with Me waits on the other side. The power of My love will put to death any hostility for others that has ruled your life. Give what you've been given, and the release of forgiveness will usher in a breakthrough of freedom that your heart has been longing for.

DAY TWENTY-NINE

He came and preached peace to you who were far away and peace to those who were near.
– Ephesians 2:17 NIV

There is no peace apart from Me; no matter how far you stray, My peace extends to cover you. Anxiousness rages in your mind, body and soul, but My peace can penetrate the whole of You. It does no good having peace of mind while your soul quakes in fear; and nothing is gained by resting your body if your mind is churning.

I am speaking peace over you regardless of your genetic history. Do you come from a bloodline of worriers? Are you the first generation to acknowledge Me as Lord? These things have no bearing on the open access you have to My peace now. So wherever you are, whatever you come from, I draw you near through My peace. Let go of your "outsized" sense of responsibility and become like a weaned child, fully content on its mother's lap. You are safe and fully supplied. I will remove all anxiousness, agitation and fear if you will simply trust Me.

DAY THIRTY

For through him we both have access to the Father by one Spirit.
— *Ephesians 2:18 NIV*

My child, I hold nothing back from you. You have been granted full access to My Presence because of the redemption offered through My Son. There remains no hindrance to coming fully into My presence. Anything that would cause you to hesitate in coming to Me is based on a lie and not the truth that I have declared.

I see your need, and yet you are content to linger in the outer courts, experiencing the secondary effects of My love. My faithfulness and the things that affect your natural world show My favor and are the results of My love—but they are not the essence of My love. How I long for you to come into the inner court that I might pour the pure potency of My love into the center of your being. Then every need, every longing you have in this moment, will be satisfied by an intimate touch of My love. Open yourself fully to Me, and the longing that is so deep you have no words for will be fulfilled.

DAY THIRTY-ONE

Consequently, you are no longer foreigners and strangers, but fellow citizens with God's people and also members of his household, built on the foundation of the apostles and prophets, with Christ Jesus himself as the chief cornerstone.
– Ephesians 2:19-20 NIV

While there was a time when you were estranged from Me, you have never been a stranger to Me. I am He who knit your inner being together in your mother's womb. I am the One who knew who you were before you were conceived. It is I who have pursued you longer than you can remember. And now I rejoice to call you a member of My household, one who has the flow of My blood and is a permanent son or daughter of Mine.

This is enough to delight My heart, but there is more. I, also, have designs for your life and purposes for your time on earth, some of which will be experienced even as soon as today. Open your eyes and open your ears for what I have in store for you today. And remember, all the resources of this household are at your disposal, and My wealth is limitless. Procure provision and strength for today. Be filled with vibrant hope for tomorrow, for your inheritance is secure.

DAY THIRTY-TWO

In him the whole building is joined together and rises to become a holy temple in the Lord. And in him you too are being built together to become a dwelling in which God lives by his Spirit.
– Ephesians 2:21-22 NIV

Let nothing distract from the calling to be a dispenser of My Presence. The significance of your life centers on the deposit of My Presence in you. The depth of relationship with Me is bottomless, and I am pouring in My fullness. Through you I spread the fragrance of My life in your world.

Likewise, in your human relationships, there is an elevation of significance that comes from being united in My Spirit with those who walk beside you in faith. This unity is supernatural, a thing of My doing. Collectively, I am forming people through whom I can pour My power and presence into. This common decision to walk together in united dependence on My love is a deep, profound expression of worship. It is the way My glory will be shown to the world—how you walk together in unity.

There are things in your life that need to be surrendered more fully to the significance of My Presence deposited in you. Today I am touching relationships that need strengthening. I am giving an open door for you to do just that.

DAY THIRTY-THREE

For this reason I, Paul, the prisoner of Christ Jesus for the sake of you Gentiles—Surely you have heard about the administration of God's grace that was given to me for you, that is, the mystery made known to me by revelation, as I have already written briefly.
– Ephesians 3:1-3 NIV

Since the day My Son suffered to bring salvation to the world, many others have joyfully and willingly suffered that My Gospel would be made known to you. Down through the ages, My people have suffered persecution, martyrdom, social separation and family isolation so that the power of My Gospel could be revealed to you. Even in your own generation, many have suffered emotional burdens as they interceded for you to come to know the mystery of Christ and the salvation that is now yours.

Let humble gratitude well up in your heart as you observe their labor has not been in vain—for you are living fruit. Their call is now your call, for I have others chosen to know the life that waits for them. I am calling you from among many to accept this ministry to your generation. I am calling you to speak My Word, to love with abandon, and to fervently intercede for those in your world that I am reaching out to. Accept the call to be My ambassadors with great joy, for many will come to know the freedom of salvation as you answer My call on your life.

As you consider this, remember what is true, that My will for your life is good, pleasing and perfect. This, then, is not a burden placed on you, but rather, the favor and blessing of My life flowing through you. You stand where you are in My Spirit today because of the sacrifice of others in your life. Remember them with thanksgiving, and accept the grace I am giving you for others that they might be saved.

DAY THIRTY-FOUR

In reading this, then, you will be able to understand my insight into the mystery of Christ, which was not made known to people in other generations as it has now been revealed by the Spirit to God's holy apostles and prophets.
– Ephesians 3:4-5 NIV

My precious child, I want you to know there are deep, profound mysteries I am revealing in the intricacy of your heart. The secrets I speak exceed the capacity of your mind to comprehend, for it is with the heart they are grasped. So intimate and expansive are the things I'm speaking that they exceed human language. Only the language of the Spirit can express what your heart is coming to understand.

Therefore, I am asking you to pursue the language I am speaking to your heart. It is here I have placed hunger and desire for the deep mysteries of My Spirit. It is with your heart that you delight in Me and experience My delight in you. I will hold nothing back from a heart that pursues the deep things that I have placed in My Son, Jesus Christ.

There are treasures to be unearthed that will transform the way you perceive Me and how you live your life. Resources have been buried in your heart that will give you power to live out the destiny I am calling you into. Do not be confused by shifting emotions; keep your eyes fixed on Me, and all these things will be brought into order and clarity for you.

DAY THIRTY-FIVE

This mystery is that through the gospel the Gentiles are heirs together with Israel, members together of one body, and sharers together in the promise in Christ Jesus.
– Ephesians 3:6 NIV

Through My Son I am revealing the abundance of the inheritance that is yours. Simply open your heart to perceive and receive what has been promised you. These promises resonate in Me with an internal depth that is in contrast to the shallow, temporal promises of this world. In Jesus, I offer life that can be lived to the full. The promises of the world are fleeting happiness that comes like the morning snow and melts before the noon day. The promises of inheritance are yours today, not just in the future; however, you must come with faith, believe in Me, and the rewards I have promised will be yours.

What promise will you choose to believe today? My promise of protection against the enemy? He has been defeated and no longer holds sway over you. Will you believe My promise to be your provider? Surrender the resources you have, and discover the peace of placing provision in My hands. My promise of grace is yours today. Do not spurn My grace by withholding forgiveness of others, and openly receive the forgiveness I am pouring into your soul.

DAY THIRTY-SIX

I became a servant of this gospel by the gift of God's grace given me through the working of his power. Although I am less than the least of all the Lord's people, this grace was given me: to preach to the Gentiles the boundless riches of Christ, and to make plain to everyone the administration of this mystery, which for ages past was kept hidden in God, who created all things.
– Ephesians 3:7-9 NIV

Something is holding you back from walking fully into the call I have for your life: fear and insecurity that fall out of the lies whispered in your ear by the enemy and over the false words that have been spoken to you by others. Do you not see? Do you not sense the truth concerning the things I see in you?

I choose the lowly, not the exalted; I choose the weak, not the strong, to accomplish the great things in My kingdom. For I can take one who sees themselves as the least and, through the great power of My grace, make them the greatest in My kingdom. There is a specific release of grace that gives you the power needed to answer the call I have for your role in building My kingdom.

Though you cannot see the rich store of power that is reserved for you, I am telling you that it will be available as you walk in the things I have called you to. An expanded release of the gospel is coming, and I want you to be part of that. Stir up your faith this day to walk in the things I have chosen for you, and what is needed will be given.

DAY THIRTY-SEVEN

His intent was that now, through the church, the manifold wisdom of God should be made known to the rulers and authorities in the heavenly realms, according to his eternal purpose that he accomplished in Christ Jesus our Lord.
– *Ephesians 3:10-11 NIV*

I've taken the deep secrets of wisdom in My heart and made them known to you. They are now manifest and have become personified in the gift of My Son to this world. Inside everyone who opens themselves to Me, I plant a seed of wisdom that will grow and expand beyond human limitations of mind and heart. This gift of My heart has been given to you, not to angels, authorities or rulers in the heavenly realm.

As the dimensions of My wisdom take hold, not only is your life transformed, but the wisdom and knowledge of My Son is revealed throughout earth and heaven. There is a concussion in the heavens, a shaking of what is falsely called wise, when My people unite and walk out the manifold wisdom that I have revealed in My Son.

What have I revealed to you that will tangibly affect the way you live your life today? Do not judge its effect by what your eyes can see and your ears can hear, but understand this—what you do resonates in the unseen realm of heaven. My glory is revealed in you and through you.

DAY THIRTY-EIGHT

In him and through faith in him we may approach God with freedom and confidence. I ask you, therefore, not to be discouraged because of my sufferings for you, which are your glory.
– Ephesians 3:12-13 NIV

One profound dimension of the wisdom that was revealed in My Son is this: while on earth, He lived in unbroken relational connection with Me, His Father. This provided the resource of His freedom, confidence and ultimate victory. Because of that victory, the same relationship is available to you through faith in Me. Is your heart longing for this freedom and victory? Then open your heart in faith, and I will come to you.

I see the way your heart has been snared. But I see deeper inside of you the freedom that already exists, that you can walk in as you put your confidence Me. I see the pain that has broken your heart and bruised your soul. But I see a deeper work of healing taking place inside you. Even now I am working healing into your life, a healing I see as accomplished.

Come to Me in faith, for you have free and open access, and I will give you confidence that what I see is true. Do I speak and not act? Do I promise and not fulfill? There is not a single word I have spoken that has not come into being, and there is not a single promise I have made that I will not fulfill. I live in unapproachable light, and yet I call you to be with Me and be cleansed and comforted. Receive the provision for everything you need in life today.

DAY THIRTY-NINE

For this reason I kneel before the Father, from whom every family in heaven and on earth derives its name.
– Ephesians 3:14-15 NIV

My child, I have given you a whole new identity as My son or daughter. Your adoption into My family has been purchased and secured by My Son. Just as He referred to Me in the most intimate of terms—Abba*—so I yearn to hear your voice call to Me as your Abba. I want to have the same relationship with you I have with Him.

The implications of this truth are more powerful than you've yet to grasp. Everything I have flows to you through the reality of this new identity. That is why who you are in Me is constantly challenged by the enemy, whose lies and deceit are causing you to forget your place in My family.

Oh, that you would live in this truth today, allowing Me to pour My love, joy and peace into the very core of your being. So kneel before Me, for you have unhindered, free access to Me in heaven. But remember this also, I come intimately close to My children who humbly seek My face.

*Abba: "Daddy," "dear Father," "papa;" a term of endearment for one's father.

DAY FORTY

I pray that out of his glorious riches he may strengthen you with power through his Spirit in your inner being, so that Christ may dwell in your hearts through faith. And I pray that you, being rooted and established in love,
– Ephesians 3:16-17 NIV

My work does not begin by addressing your circumstances. The primary focus of My power is not centered on the external things of your life. The fulcrum of My power drills past all of that and pours strength into your inner being. My power manifests first in the core of your being, altering and transforming the context of your heart. My strength gives you the ability to endure whatever is taking place on the outside.

Look back on your life and remember the circumstances where you asked yourself, "How will I make it through this?" Do you know that My strength is what caused you to endure it, but more than that, grow in it? Even in the dark night of your soul, I am strengthening you by My power in your spirit.

Stir up your faith for what you face today, and My power will come pouring inside of you. Let the power of My joy transform the condition of your heart, and you will discover that from the inside out your circumstances will begin to change.

DAY FORTY-ONE

so that Christ may dwell in your hearts through faith. And I pray that you, being rooted and established in love, may have power, together with all the Lord's holy people, to grasp how wide and long and high and deep is the love of Christ,
– *Ephesians 3:17-18 NIV*

There's no other place where you can find worth and security than in My love. You cannot establish yourself through experience, for that can mislead; you cannot secure yourself to success, for that may be taken from you; nor can your life be rooted in obedience to the law, or any set of rules you have made for yourself, for that is beyond you.

I am pouring My love into you, freely and abundantly given, and no one can take it from you. My love was not earned, so there is no failure that can shake it from you. This love flows from My heart, so it roots you in what is eternal. Nothing in all of heaven and earth can threaten this foundation I have given you.

Whatever disqualifying thoughts or striving impulses you have, I will sweep aside if you will open yourself more fully to My love. In place of these, I will give the peace of security and the confidence of being established in My love, which is eternally yours.

DAY FORTY-TWO

...may have power, together with all the Lord's holy people, to grasp how wide and long and high and deep is the love of Christ, and to know this love that surpasses knowledge—that you may be filled to the measure of all the fullness of God.
– Ephesians 3:18-19 NIV

My love for you is deeper and richer than any human being in themselves could possibly grasp. It is attainable only through the power of My Spirit manifested in you, giving the ability to go beyond your boundaries to experience the fullness of My love.

I am taking you past the limitations of your mind. You rely too heavily on what you can comprehend and think through. My love for you supersedes intellect. To experience My love, you must move beyond the barriers of trust that fear has erected. The ones who have broken trust through unfulfilled promises do not represent Me. I have gone to great lengths to secure your trust through My Son. Let go of fear, and trust Me fully, so you may experience the depth of My love.

I am altogether good, capable of taking everything in your life and working it for your good. Your reluctance to accept the complete goodness of My character inhibits your experience of My love. My Spirit is ready to fill you with the fullness of My love. Trust in My goodness, relinquish your fears, and rest your mind so that you may encounter Me at a level never before known to you.

DAY FORTY-THREE

Now to him who is able to do immeasurably more than all we ask or imagine, according to his power that is at work within us, to him be glory in the church and in Christ Jesus throughout all generations, for ever and ever! Amen.
– Ephesians 3:20-21 NIV

Listen to me, My child. If you could comprehend the incredible strength of My power at work, in you and for you, then you would not fear the future. This power is released exponentially, in increasing measure, as you cultivate belief by faith in what is unseen, not by sight, and what you think is true.

Your future seems tightly controlled, wrapped up in the neat little plans that you have made. I am asking you to release control and trust Me. The things I have in store for you are too wonderful for you to comprehend now. In this day-by-day unveiling, opportunities and possibilities that could not possibly have been known by you will miraculously appear. These are the plans I have prepared in advance for you, and they are discovered as you are made ready.

DAY FORTY-FOUR

As a prisoner for the Lord, then, I urge you to live a life worthy of the calling you have received.
– Ephesians 4:1 NIV

I am giving you peace, provision and passion for the calling I have on your life. Keep yourself centered and focused on this calling, which is uniquely yours. You ask, "What is this calling?" and you become weary in striving and running after the things you think I'm asking you to do. Beloved, My calling is right in front of you. It is not so much the things you must do—that comes later as an outgrowth of My primary calling—it is being the person I've made you to be.

Discover who I have made you to be, and there you will find My calling on your life. So much of My peace is lost in your attempt to be something that you are not; or you wish to do something for Me I have not asked of you. Rest secure in the person you are in Me, and the things I have for you to do will become self-evident. Be at peace in the knowledge that I have given you the provision and the ability to enter into all of the calling I have for you.

DAY FORTY-FIVE

Be completely humble and gentle; be patient, bearing with one another in love.
– Ephesians 4:2 NIV

Humility is a key to advancing in Me. This was modeled by My Son. Humility brought you to salvation as you confessed your brokenness and weakness. The continuation of the way you began in Me leads to your advancement in Me.

Every last remnant of pride must go, for it is the bondage of your past life. You must wage war against this old enemy, which is the foundation of all darkness and evil. The work of darkness was broken when humility led My Son to the cross. Humility gives permission for My light and life to flood into every situation. In this way, humility becomes the key to opening up the relationships you have on earth. There are relationships in your life where pride has created tension, brought conflict and caused pain.

I am asking you, first, to humble yourself before Me, then I will pour out for you the resources you need for these relationships. Humble yourself before others, live with patience and forbearance, and I will cause the relationships in your life to flourish and be made whole.

DAY FORTY-SIX

Make every effort to keep the unity of the Spirit through the bond of peace.
– Ephesians 4:3 NIV

The unity you crave with My people comes first from your union with Me. The ensuing peace that flows from your relationship with Me is an indicator that you and I have become one. All agitation, indignation and yes, even injustice, you must lay at My feet, relieving yourself of its burden. Only then can you participate in the unity I am bringing to the church.

If you seek peace only through relationships in My Body, your peace is built on shaky ground. But when your peace flows from the unity of My spirit, then the miraculous work established on a solid foundation comes into being. I am your unity; I am your peace. The necessity of what you personally lay down to walk in that unity with Me fosters the peace I offer—these are the same ingredients necessary to walk in unity with others.

Disunity from your past has hurt you, and the pain still infects your life in Me to this day. Lay down your pain, and come to Me. Present yourself to be united with Me, and the balm of peace will be the healing that binds your wounds. You will then see a supernatural unity established between you and others who walk together under My Lordship.

DAY FORTY-SEVEN

There is one body and one Spirit, just as you were called to one hope when you were called; one Lord, one faith, one baptism;
– Ephesians 4:4-6 NIV

Beloved, I see confusion in you. There is a mix of false and conflicting allegiances in your heart. You say I am Lord, and this is primarily true, but there are many secondary lords to which you, knowingly and unknowingly, give authority in your life. Work, people, things and circumstances are some of the things My people submit themselves to which create confusion about who is in control of their lives. These things pose great risk to you. They sow confusion about your purpose, who you are and what is important in your life.

I see how consuming these other things can be, but I tell you this: I am Lord of it all. Hope awaits when you release control and fully submit all of these things to My Lordship. I have tremendous plans I am working out on your behalf. Will you trust Me in all of these secondary areas and cease looking to exert control over these arenas?

Nothing escapes My notice; My focus is on you, and My desire is to pour blessing and favor upon you in every aspect of your life. If you will sever the secondary allegiances, you will find more life in Me, and your joy will be increased and released to the fullest extent in you.

DAY FORTY-EIGHT

But to each one of us grace has been given as Christ apportioned it.
– Ephesians 4:7 NIV

You have experienced and recognize My grace in the forgiveness of your sin and the strength to cover your weaknesses. My grace is available to cover your shortcomings, but it is so much more than that. My grace takes you beyond yourself in the things that are too big for you.

Where have you sensed My call and said, "That's too much for me"? Or what circumstance have you faced and said, "This is too big for me"? Know this, My child: I will not allow a circumstance in your life and not sufficiently supply the grace you need to walk through it. Nor will I call you into service and leave you in your own strength. No, rather, I will abundantly supply the resource you need to do the service I've asked.

So take hope, for even now My grace is pouring out in sufficient supply for whatever is in front of you. Though you may not see it with your eyes or feel it with your emotions, receive it in faith. The course of your life is covered by My grace, and this will become abundantly clear to you.

DAY FORTY-NINE

This is why it says: "When he ascended on high, he took many captives and gave gifts to his people." (What does "he ascended" mean except that he also descended to the lower, earthly regions? He who descended is the very one who ascended higher than all the heavens, in order to fill the whole universe.)
– *Ephesians 4:8-10 NIV*

Consider the great lengths to which I go to secure the ones that are mine. There is no place so dark or so deep to which I will not descend in order to rescue you and release you into freedom. I will not leave you there when I find you but will lift you up into the high places of heaven with Me. There I will shower you with gifts that are unique and personally fitted just for you.

My enemy desires to snuff out the grand purposes I have for you, but he will not succeed if you trust in Me, for he has no authority. Consider these gifts I have given which enable you to walk in all the things I have for you. Do not consider them in human terms, but in great hope, see these gifts as they are: supernatural provision for you.

This is so much grander than you realize, for My plan is to bring all who call on My name into heavenly places and, there, pour My glory into them. In this way, you are part of the whole universe being filled with My glory. How will you live today in light of this glorious knowledge?

DAY FIFTY

So Christ himself gave the apostles, the prophets, the evangelists, the pastors and teachers, to equip his people for works of service, so that the body of Christ may be built up until we all reach unity in the faith and in the knowledge of the Son of God and become mature, attaining to the whole measure of the fullness of Christ.
– Ephesians 4:11-13 NIV

None of My followers can advance in Me without the maturing effect of a healthy church. There is no plausible rationale to live in isolation and loneliness as a follower of mine. I have put leaders in place to cover you and have drawn comrades full of My Spirit to surround you. Leadership is established by Me, and the Body has been given gifts, service and supernatural gifts so that the full maturity and unique calling I have for each individual would be realized.

I am calling you into this Spirit-filled community where all the resources I have given surround you. When you engage with My Body, not only do you benefit, but you become a significant part of My church so all may attain the whole measure of My fullness.

DAY FIFTY-ONE

Then we will no longer be infants, tossed back and forth by the waves, and blown here and there by every wind of teaching and by the cunning and craftiness of people in their deceitful scheming.
– Ephesians 4:14 NIV

For too long your life has been dominated by the opinion of others, things that have been said or things that haven't been said. The result has been spiritual and emotional upheaval in your life. It's time that you learn to walk in the fullness of the measure of maturity I am giving you.

I am teaching you to hear My voice and distinguish it from the other voices that you've grown accustomed to listening to. Well-intentioned people have spoken things over you or requested things of you, but I am teaching you to filter every other voice but Mine. Meditate on what I am speaking out of My Word and the whisper of My Spirit, then surrender yourself to My authority. I will direct you on a solid path; I will straighten out the crooked places and impart a peaceful plan for the days ahead. Do you hear My voice speaking to you today?

DAY FIFTY-TWO

Instead, speaking the truth in love, we will grow to become in every respect the mature body of him who is the head, that is, Christ.
– *Ephesians 4:15 NIV*

Your assignment today is to immerse yourself in My love. All of the urgent things your mind turns to, all the pressing issues demanding your attention, are secondary to this. It only takes a moment to remember you are secure in the love that I have and allow it to surround you.

From this place of love, I give you the courage and resources to accomplish what I am asking of you today. This means some of the urgent and pressing things will fall away, for they are not meant for today. Look for moments in your day when My love urges you to speak truthfully to others. I am preparing you for this. For some, it means courageously speaking the truth about what I am asking of you and how they will be affected. For others it means tenderly speaking the loving, affirming words that have been in your heart but have remained unspoken.

Let My love flow from your heart, through your lips, to the people in your world…a gift given to others by Me and through you, born out of your choice to be immersed in My love right now.

DAY FIFTY-THREE

From him the whole body, joined and held together by every supporting ligament, grows and builds itself up in love, as each part does its work.
– Ephesians 4:16 NIV

Often My love is released in you for your comfort. But today I am releasing My love for your strengthening. As you open up and allow My love to drive deep inside, your faith will be strengthened and the measure of your trust increased.

This process causes you to grow and builds up the measure of My fullness within you. It is out of this place that I ask you to walk in the things I have assigned for you. As you exercise the gifts and abilities that have been given through the Spirit, others will be built up and strengthened in My love.

Do not believe the lie whispering in your ear that you are inconsequential. No one who is grown and built up in My love is inconsequential. I have prepared, in advance, a part for you to play. Would I do so and not provide what you need to complete it? Do not let this lie inflict paralysis, for the whole body suffers when you do. I am strengthening and releasing you today, that you might give away what I have given to you. And yes, even in this you are strengthened further by My love.

DAY FIFTY-FOUR

So I tell you this, and insist on it in the Lord, that you must no longer live as the Gentiles do, in the futility of their thinking. They are darkened in their understanding and separated from the life of God because of the ignorance that is in them due to the hardening of their hearts.
– Ephesians 4:17-18 NIV

There are areas of your lifestyle that remain untouched by My light. Some of these you are aware of, and they are too precious for you to let go of. Other areas are shameful and abhorrent, yet you seem to be powerless. This behavior finds its energy in soul-level lies and wounds.

I have seen the extent of effort you have made to change your behavior, and each time you've asked for forgiveness, I have given it. The real issue is not about unforgiven sin. It is good that you resist this behavior, but these patterns are not easily addressed by the sheer force of your will. It is far more important that you surrender to My life and light these deep areas where your behavior finds its source.

Allow My Spirit to penetrate the dark areas of your soul and, there, I will infuse you with My life and strength. The more your soul is exposed to My light, the more transformation that will come in the way you live. Right now, still your heart before Me, and I will bring clarity to you about this. In this moment, I am touching these places. Open your mind and your heart to My life and light.

DAY FIFTY-FIVE

Having lost all sensitivity, they have given themselves over to sensuality so as to indulge in every kind of impurity, and they are full of greed. That, however, is not the way of life you learned when you heard about Christ and were taught in him in accordance with the truth that is in Jesus.
– Ephesians 4:19-21 NIV

Dear one, when you accepted the gift of My Son, the Spirit of Truth came to live in the core of your being. My truth takes the fragmented, scattered thoughts and ideas that divide your heart and unites them with Mine. My truth sets you free from the cyclical patterns of darkness that can imprison you. My truth breaks the behavioral ruts in which you are stuck. My Spirit of Truth penetrates deception and exposes lies, allowing you to walk in freedom.

Meditate on the truth of My Word, enjoy the presence of My Spirit of Truth, and you will find the life you long for is within reach. I will go with you today as your guide so you will not lose your way.

DAY FIFTY-SIX

You were taught, with regard to your former way of life, to put off your old self, which is being corrupted by its deceitful desires; to be made new in the attitude of your minds; and to put on the new self, created to be like God in true righteousness and holiness.
– Ephesians 4:22-24 NIV

The person you were before My Spirit remade you is dead. The focus of your life is now learning to walk in a way consistent with the new person you are. There are impulses and habits that still affect your life from the old person you were. But like muscle memory, which causes a dead body to move, these things will fade with time, and the new person I've made you to be will take over.

You are not left alone in this process, for I have given you My Spirit. This new person you are is being given a renewed mind, one that thinks My thoughts and knows what I know. This new attitude of the mind stimulates your heart to feel what I feel, want what I desire.

Stop and listen to My thoughts right now. Take this moment to meditate on what I desire, for I am revealing it to you even now. In this way, My Spirit exerts dominion in you and brings Me glory when you more fully become the new creation I have made you to be.

DAY FIFTY-SEVEN

Therefore each of you must put off falsehood and speak truthfully to your neighbor, for we are all members of one body. "In your anger do not sin"[a]: Do not let the sun go down while you are still angry, and do not give the devil a foothold.
– Ephesians 4:25-27 NIV

Beloved, it is My desire that you flourish relationally in your life. This happens best when there is mutual honor one for another. I am asking you to come in line with My creative design in regard to relationships: one important aspect is showing honor to the people around you. Truthful speech honors; falsehood dishonors. Relationships benefit from truthful words spoken in the context of love.

You were not designed to withstand an accumulated burden of anger and bitterness. Not only are you physically harmed, but this creates an open door for spiritual harm as well. Burying the pain inflicted by another without an attempt to gain understanding and healing dishonors them; the pursuit of reconciliation and mutual relationship honors them. My heart hurts for the pain you have received from others, but understand this: the extent to which you bury feelings, withhold emotion, and placate one another increases the risk of damage and harm.

Release and healing come when you let go of anger through the pursuit of truth and openness. What relationship comes to mind? That is My spirit urging you to pursue this path to a relationship that flourishes.

[a] Psalm 4:4

DAY FIFTY-EIGHT

Anyone who has been stealing must steal no longer, but must work, doing something useful with their own hands, that they may have something to share with those in need.
— *Ephesians 4:28 NIV*

As My children, you are to emulate Me: My character, My love, My grace and My generosity. This means living your life on earth with a generous spirit toward others. I am your provider, not only to supply your needs but, also, to provide an ability to live as an agent of My generosity in your world.

For some, I have given financial abundance: look for ways I am leading you to share it. By My grace, all of you have been given an abundance of joy: be an encouragement to those who are in a place of struggle today. Many of you, through My spirit, have been given strength of heart and emotional wellbeing. This, too, I am asking you to share with others to bring strength and stability to them during a time of stress that threatens to drown them in pain and grief.

As you increase in your faith and willingness to share what I've given you, more will be made available by My Spirit. Your generosity is a key component in reaching the full stature of maturity that I have given to you. Be alert as you walk through these coming days, for I am bringing into your life those in need.

DAY FIFTY-NINE

Do not let any unwholesome talk come out of your mouths, but only what is helpful for building others up according to their needs, that it may benefit those who listen. And do not grieve the Holy Spirit of God, with whom you were sealed for the day of redemption.

– Ephesians 4:29-30 NIV

My Spirit, which is the source of your new self, has been placed as a foundation for this life I am giving you. In My Spirit, this new life has been sealed and secured for the future I have planned for you.

Now a choice has been given to you. Will you lead with your own will and soul or allow My Spirit to lead by giving Me center stage in your life? I can give you the ability to allow the life I have given you to flow out to others you encounter. I am giving you words to speak that will cut to their core and bring encouragement in a dark world. My Spirit is giving you insight so you know the things I have placed deep inside of them and, through Me, have the power to call them into reality.

Any words contrary to My Spirit that you might speak not only cause others harm, but they diminish the life of My Spirit in you and erode My influence over you. This makes Me grieve, and it hurts you. However, if you will let Me lead, you will speak My words, though you do not know them now; and they will have an eternal impact on the people I have put in your life.

DAY SIXTY

Get rid of all bitterness, rage and anger, brawling and slander, along with every form of malice. Be kind and compassionate to one another, forgiving each other, just as in Christ God forgave you.
– Ephesians 4:31-32 NIV

Everything associated with your old life must go. These things tear at the new life of love to which I have called you. You are now Mine because of the kindness and compassion I have for you. You are now free because of My forgiveness and mercy in you. I am calling you to live a life of love—a life that shows the character I have put inside of you.

The power of My love has not only changed your life radically, but this same power will change others in the same way as it flows through you. This will cost you something: the cost of laying down your perceived right to hold onto unforgiveness toward others; the cost of a burden that you carry for the pain of others as you embody My compassion for them. Dear child, this cost comes with a significant reward as this way of life leads you into a deeper, richer way of living. It will fulfill you in a way that you cannot imagine. Make it your ambition to allow My Spirit to lead in your life.

DAY SIXTY-ONE

Follow God's example, therefore, as dearly loved children and walk in the way of love, just as Christ loved us and gave himself up for us as a fragrant offering and sacrifice to God.
– Ephesians 5:1-2 NIV

From the beginning, I CHOSE to love you. My love is established in the center of My will, stable and unchanging. It was expressed extravagantly through the sacrifice of My Son, so you might be free to choose to love Me. And now I'm asking you to love others as I have loved you.

This love begins in the center of your will; it is something you choose. My love is a part of My character, not just My emotion. Grow in My love in such a way that it becomes established in you at a character level. Emotional love, though pleasant and pleasurable at times, is fickle and insubstantial. Just as sure as it will bring you pleasure, it will also bring you pain, which causes this kind of love to dissipate. Sympathetic love may stir you to care, but when the cause for sympathy ends, the reason for its existence ceases. My love continues on, and so must yours.

Choose to love others unconditionally, and do not turn away, no matter what comes. Only then will you have come to love deeply. When you love in this way, you show yourself to be My child, and the world will see that you are Mine.

DAY SIXTY-TWO

But among you there must not be even a hint of sexual immorality, or of any kind of impurity, or of greed, because these are improper for God's holy people. Nor should there be obscenity, foolish talk or coarse joking, which are out of place, but rather thanksgiving. For of this you can be sure: No immoral, impure or greedy person—such a person is an idolater—has any inheritance in the kingdom of Christ and of God. Let no one deceive you with empty words, for because of such things God's wrath comes on those who are disobedient. Therefore do not be partners with them.
– Ephesians 5:3-7 NIV

Though the fullness of My kingdom has yet to be realized, it is even now breaking through in your life. The blessings of My kingdom include peace, joy and open relationship with Me based on My righteousness given you. This is available for those who choose Me and pursue Me.

Even though you stumble, I will not let you fall, for your heart is turned toward Me and humbly seeks Me. Yet, if you harden your heart and turn away, rejecting My kingdom, you open yourself up to the kingdom of darkness. When you say "no" to Me and the kingdom of light, you have said "yes" to the kingdom of darkness. Now the aspects and attributes of that kingdom will begin to dominate your life: immorality, which is the craving to fulfill oneself without regard to what is right and wrong; impurity, which longs for things it shouldn't have, that seem alluring but quickly turn to bitterness in the aftermath; greed, the perpetual, insatiable desire for more of what the world might offer that leads to deep dissatisfaction.

Upon the proud, arrogant and rebellious, I will not force My kingdom, so the devastating consequence is that darkness rules over them. But not so with you, for to the humble, contrite and thankful, I make everything I have, My full inheritance, available to satisfy and fulfill every longing.

Do you feel weak in your resistance to the pull of this world? Remember and be thankful for all that I have done for you, reciting to Me the gratitude of your heart. In doing this, the delusion of the enemy will be broken, and the beauty of My kingdom will shine through.

DAY SIXTY-THREE

For you were once darkness, but now you are light in the Lord. Live as children of light (for the fruit of the light consists in all goodness, righteousness and truth) and find out what pleases the Lord.
– Ephesians 5:8-10 NIV

My will for you today is that you expose every shadowed area of your heart to My light. As My child, it pleases Me when you willingly, transparently open yourself up in My presence. Just as nocturnal creatures in the natural world scatter when exposed to light, so things associated with spiritual darkness flee under the scrutiny of My light.

While you warm yourself in My presence today, I will show you the multi-dimensional measure of My goodness toward you. On one level, My goodness spreads broadly over the whole world and encompasses your life. At another level, and this is what you need to hear in this season, My goodness is very specific to you. I have poured it out in tangible and supernatural ways that are tailor-made for you. But I am not done: I have plans to continue bringing My goodness in unique ways that line up with My will for you.

As you bask in My goodness, you will come to know what pleases Me. When you, as My child, live in My light filled with all righteousness, all goodness and all truth, it pleases Me and gives life to you. The more you grasp of My goodness, the clearer your understanding of what gives Me pleasure.

DAY SIXTY-FOUR

Have nothing to do with the fruitless deeds of darkness, but rather expose them. It is shameful even to mention what the disobedient do in secret. But everything exposed by the light becomes visible—and everything that is illuminated becomes a light. This is why it is said: "Wake up, sleeper, rise from the dead, and Christ will shine on you."
– Ephesians 5:11-14 NIV

There is a deep drowsiness that pervades this world which can weigh heavily on the eyes of your spirit. When the light that I put within you begins to dim or fade for lack of attention, too much distraction or busyness, spiritual slumber begins to creep in. The ground that has been taken over by My light remains exposed and revealed.

It is so easy to be lulled to sleep by what your physical senses perceive. What your ears hear, what your eyes take in and what stimulates your mind, if dominated by this world, can bring about spiritual inertia. Even the physical comfort your body craves can numb you into believing that the physical senses are of primary importance.

Don't be fooled for a second; and don't wait for a crisis to expose this slow creep of slumber entering your life. Allow Me to shake you from your sleep even now. The things most vibrant and alive lie unseen to the natural eyes and unheard by the natural ears. Hear My clarion call to awake so My life will become acute and real to you. In this alert spiritual state, eternity lies before you,

continued on next page....

and the abundance of My life pours in. Do the work, take the time, be in My light, allow it to penetrate every part of you. Then you will walk through this day as one who is fully awake in Me.

DAY SIXTY-FIVE

Be very careful, then, how you live—not as unwise but as wise, making the most of every opportunity, because the days are evil. Therefore do not be foolish, but understand what the Lord's will is.
– Ephesians 5:15-17 NIV

As you live your life alert and awake in Me, keep a careful eye out for the opportunities that I am bringing to you. Not a day goes by where I have not positioned you strategically and given you the portion of wisdom needed to infuse a situation with My presence and bring it into alignment with My will.

Pay careful attention, for these opportunities can easily be overlooked if you allow yourself to become too busy and preoccupied. Resist the temptation to foolishly chase after the things of this world. I am showing you a life worth chasing after. Each day will bring moments pregnant with possibility to live in My will in these evil days and people to love, in word and deed, whom I am in process of rescuing. This is My will, that your life be fraught with purpose, filled with the wisdom and lived full of the love that comes from Me.

DAY SIXTY-SIX

Do not get drunk on wine, which leads to debauchery. Instead, be filled with the Spirit, speaking to one another with psalms, hymns, and songs from the Spirit. Sing and make music from your heart to the Lord, always giving thanks to God the Father for everything, in the name of our Lord Jesus Christ.
– Ephesians 5:18-20 NIV

There are many things you can be filled with that numb your mind and bring confusion. My desire is to fill your life with My Spirit; and this is not a one-time event, but an ongoing, daily filling. Through My Spirit, I will bring clarity of mind and order to your soul.

Release the flow of My Spirit by singing songs, reciting My Word and speaking in the spiritual language which I have given you. Do this when you are alone and as you gather with My people, and I will visit you with power and authority and strength. And in everything be thankful; thanksgiving is a sure catalyst for the release of My Spirit, and it comes from a clear mind, able to see the good things I am doing in your life.

DAY SIXTY-SEVEN

Submit to one another out of reverence for Christ.
– Ephesians 5:21 NIV

My child, as you seek to advance in Me, one of the keys that you will discover is the importance of submission under My authority. This is a safe place of protection and an avenue of blessing for your life. As you learn the rhythm of walking in submission, you will discover that this extends as a blessing into all of your relationships. Though they may not have authority over you, the humility required to walk in submission opens a dimension of My love and your love for others that could not be accessed another way.

As your trust in Me grows, you will see the favor I bring into your life as you learn to live out My divine order established for you. As you trust in Me, you will come to see that there are those who walk in My Spirit you can trust as well. In that mutual submission, a love is fostered that the world cannot know or understand. There is security, acceptance and favor that come from this place of trust.

DAY SIXTY-EIGHT

Wives, submit yourselves to your own husbands as you do to the Lord. For the husband is the head of the wife as Christ is the head of the church, his body, of which he is the Savior. Now as the church submits to Christ, so also wives should submit to their husbands in everything.
– Ephesians 5:22-24 NIV

Now open your heart to a fresh revelation of My love over your life. I have buried a picture of divine love in the most intimate and trusting of human relationships. When I create a whole, healthy and secure marriage, the bond of unity between a man and a woman tells the story of My love over and over again. In this picture, the husband emulates My character—love, trustworthiness, faithfulness, kindness, humility—while taking the lead in establishing these traits in the relationship. The wife responds to his leadership by following in trusting submission.

In this divine order, the wife follows the husband, the husband fully submits to Me, and each submits to one another under Me. This order is paramount for the full blessing of My love to flow unimpeded. A supernatural relational dynamic is created that opens the most intimate and mutually-satisfying marriage possible.

What I am describing is only available to those who recognize their need for My power and humbly submit to My authority. I am waiting to pour My favor into your life, but you must lay down what has hindered you regarding My divine order and trust Me fully. Through marriage, I proclaim My love to a world starving for secure acceptance and unconditional love.

DAY SIXTY-NINE

Husbands, love your wives, just as Christ loved the church and gave himself up for her to make her holy, cleansing her by the washing with water through the word, and to present her to himself as a radiant church, without stain or wrinkle or any other blemish, but holy and blameless.
– Ephesians 5:25-27 NIV

I am asking all of you husbands to lead in the way of My Spirit. Lead in the way of forgiveness and truth so that you and your wife can live free, holy and blameless before Me. Lead in the way of My love, first by learning to be loved fully by Me. As you encounter My love, you will be able to love like Me.

I have designed husbands to be more than responders. Generations of abdication must be confronted and overcome. Do not follow the path of your fathers, but learn from Me how to love and lead in relationship. The depths of love and richness of relationship will only be discovered as you follow My ways.

Do you feel broken and inadequate today? Then come to Me; I will cleanse you with the blood of My Son, and I will restore you with the power of My Spirit so that you can rise up and become the man that I have intended you to be.

DAY SEVENTY

In this same way, husbands ought to love their wives as their own bodies. He who loves his wife loves himself. After all, no one ever hated their own body, but they feed and care for their body, just as Christ does the church—for we are members of his body.
– Ephesians 5:28-30 NIV

Today I want to address the shallow form of love that is birthed out of deep insecurity. This love has no substance and is given, not for the intended object of love, but as a means to earn favor, gain recognition or garner attention. It is an attempt to assuage the painful inner view, the self-loathing of who you perceive yourself to be. You are only partially aware of these emotions, but they run deeper than you know. The enemy has twisted words, skewed experiences and imposed deep regret, using them to warp your perspective of yourself.

Who would hate their own body? It seems obvious that no one should, yet many do. Who can truly love from that place of self-hatred? Let these words penetrate your soul: I created you and love you deeply; nothing you can do will change that. I am restoring you and call you My own.

When you look in the mirror, think My thoughts: "This is one who is dearly loved by God." Allow Me to cleanse the self-despite from your eyes, and encounter My love. Only from that place of encounter can you love truly—a love that is no longer just an empty form, but a permanent substance; a love like Mine.

DAY SEVENTY-ONE

"For this reason a man will leave his father and mother and be united to his wife, and the two will become one flesh."[a] This is a profound mystery—but I am talking about Christ and the church. However, each one of you also must love his wife as he loves himself, and the wife must respect her husband.
– *Ephesians 5:31-33 NIV*

The message I speak through marriage is of intimate love between Me and you. Consider and understand this: the natural flows out of what is supernatural. There is a divine story of love in which you play an integral part. The level of affection, love and intimacy between you and Me requires that you leave everything that you depend on and place your dependence solely on Me.

In marriage, a man and woman leave the comfortable dependence of parents in order to form a new union. So it is that in divine love, the former things that brought security, some of them good in their season, must be left behind so you may cling to Me, trust in Me and be dependent on Me.

Just as unity is expressed between a man and woman through physical union, so you are united with Me as I live in you and you in Me. Unless a person enters into this supernatural reality, the full satisfaction intended for marriage cannot be attained. Your love for Me grows in the fertile soil of love, respect and honor. This is, also, true of the love between a man and woman.

[a] Genesis 2:24

DAY SEVENTY-TWO

Children, obey your parents in the Lord, for this is right. "Honor your father and mother"—which is the first commandment with a promise—"so that it may go well with you and that you may enjoy long life on the earth."[a]
– Ephesians 6:1-3 NIV

Dear child on whom My favor rests, I have given you divine keys that unlock blessings which have been stored up for you. Honor is an important key in all relationships but most significant in regard to a child with a parent. Your decision to show honor triggers My favor and full enjoyment of life in Me.

Honor is given rather than earned, for it lies within the choice of the giver, not the receiver. Through your will, you can choose to honor in spite of things that would inhibit that expression. Honor changes the dynamic of a relationship, allowing health to come where there has been brokenness. In the backdrop of every healthy relationship is mutual honor. Choose to honor your father and mother or, if necessary, their memory. If you do this, I will release My favor and blessing into your life, extending to your children. The honor you show teaches this divine key to the next generation.

[a] Deuteronomy 5:16

DAY SEVENTY-THREE

Fathers, do not exasperate your children; instead, bring them up in the training and instruction of the Lord.

– Ephesians 6:4 NIV

I am instructing and training you in the way that leads to joy, peace and freedom. The boundaries that have been set around you are a loving means of protection, given by Me to establish a loving order. Understanding this breeds an atmosphere of freedom, love and security.

What is true for you is true for those I've placed under your care. Do not set boundaries out of fear, and do not react out of anger, for that pollutes the atmosphere I am seeking to establish in your home. The imprint of your care opens their spirit to Me and increases their ability to receive My love.

This is especially true for fathers and children. Learn to care for your children in the same way I care for you. Through My Spirit, I am giving everything you need for your assigned role, particularly love, goodness, patience, gentleness, self-control. Lean into Me, and you will find your resource. Teach them what I have taught you, with the same gentleness and grace, then you will find a heart that responds to your care. Negative parental patterns can change now by My power. If you will persevere in this, I will restore what has been lost.

DAY SEVENTY-FOUR

Slaves, obey your earthly masters with respect and fear, and with sincerity of heart, just as you would obey Christ. Obey them not only to win their favor when their eye is on you, but as slaves of Christ, doing the will of God from your heart. Serve wholeheartedly, as if you were serving the Lord, not people, because you know that the Lord will reward each one for whatever good they do, whether they are slave or free.
– Ephesians 6:5-8 NIV

Buried deep inside you, I have placed the need to serve and be productive. Whether you will serve is not an option, but who you serve is. When you serve Me with a cheerful heart, no matter what your station in life, you will find your fullest satisfaction. When you recognize that everything you do is an active service to Me, you will find advancement in My kingdom.

However, there are other masters you may choose to serve. This kind of service exposes you to potential pain and heartache, for no other master is as kind and benevolent as Me. You may be trapped in service to a goal which enslaves you or be mistreated by a person who controls you. Do you serve money, employers or pleasure? This will lead to disillusionment and destructive behavior. In some cases the pain is obvious, but in others it is a more subtle deception. In either case, you may only serve ONE master—so choose Me.

When you willingly and knowingly serve Me in whatever circumstance you are in, I am free to release favor and reward into your life. Divine blessing is released in you, first impacting your inner world and then working its way out into the external circumstance. Any master that dominates your life apart from Me poses great risk to you. My power is available for breaking this poisonous influence over you, that you might serve Me alone.

DAY SEVENTY-FIVE

And masters, treat your slaves in the same way. Do not threaten them, since you know that he who is both their Master and yours is in heaven, and there is no favoritism with him.
– Ephesians 6:9 NIV

There are people in your world I have asked you to lead, individuals I've given you a measure of authority over. They look to you for wisdom, guidance and provision. Never forget this: both you and they are fully, equally under My authority and rule. My authority is never selfish, never rude and never harsh. I always look for ways to use My influence to bring about good things for those under My care. So must you.

First, recognize the people I've placed in your life to lead. Second, remember that all are equal in My eyes and deserving of My love, affection and grace. Then, finally, learn the model of authority and leadership I have shown. If you wish to lead, you must first learn to selflessly serve those under your care. I am showing you ways to serve in your leadership role. Consider the multiplied impact that following My model will have. In so doing, I will cause both you and those you serve to come fully into the purposes I have for your lives.

DAY SEVENTY-SIX

Finally, be strong in the Lord and in his mighty power.
– Ephesians 6:10 NIV

You want so much to be strong, but time and again you exhaust yourself colliding with your human frailty and physical limitations. Spent and desperate, you cry out to Me for strength you know I can give. Beloved, the strength you ask for is not the strength you need, for it does not emanate from My power. You misunderstand how My power works. The strength I give is not to fuel your own endurance and sufficiency. That would only encourage exhausting yourself further . . . physically, emotionally and mentally.

The full extent of My power is given to those who have come to the end of themselves and realize that nothing can be accomplished in their own strength. My power comes in and surprises, because the things I desire are accomplished not by power in the natural but in spite of the natural weakness you have viewed as a hindrance. Cease striving to be strong in yourself and avoiding weakness. Do you feel weak? Good! Finally, you can now be strong in Me.

Watch for My power to surprise you, for I manifest most fully in those who are comfortable with their own limitations. My might is on display in a life that recognizes human strength as a deterrent to seeing the powerful work I have planned to accomplish. Choose today to stand in the tension between your own limitations and My unlimited power made available to those who believe.

DAY SEVENTY-SEVEN

Put on the full armor of God, so that you can take your stand against the devil's schemes. For our struggle is not against flesh and blood, but against the rulers, against the authorities, against the powers of this dark world and against the spiritual forces of evil in the heavenly realms.
– Ephesians 6:11-12 NIV

Today you will face troubles and difficulties that seem to be originating through people or physical circumstances. This is not true, My child, for everything finds its origins in the spiritual realm. So your struggles are, ultimately, an attempt by the enemy to infuse doubt, discouragement and darkness in and upon you.

Take courage in this: I have overcome all the authorities and powers of that dark world as well as the troubles you face in your earthly life. This victory is yours when I clothe you with My power from on high. I am giving you tailor-made weapons and protection from anything you may face.

It is important you understand that, though people and circumstance assail you, My power is strong enough to guard and care for the precious life I have given you. The physical struggles are surface, the spiritual challenges are deep, but there is no power strong enough to overcome the salvation, peace, love and joy I have placed in you if you remain covered by My power. Apprehend all I have given you so that you will stand in My strength and authority.

DAY SEVENTY-EIGHT

Therefore put on the full armor of God, so that when the day of evil comes, you may be able to stand your ground, and after you have done everything, to stand.
– Ephesians 6:13 NIV

The war against evil has been fought and victoriously won by My Son; therefore, the ultimate outcome for you is certain. However, while you linger on earth, the battle against evil continues to rage. Never doubt that I have given you everything necessary to remain immovable when you are attacked. I am giving you divine weapons and protection fashioned for spiritual warfare.

Do not think this will pass you by, for the assault by the evil one attempts to engulf all whom I have created. You are not to tremble nor be afraid, for no evil weapon formed against you will have success when you are enclosed in My protection. On the contrary, I have given divine weapons with power to push back darkness and take ground for My kingdom. Be alert and prepared with awareness, for passivity plays into the enemy's plans. Take up the weapons I have given and, by faith, cover yourself in the protection I have provided. You will need these things each day more than you know.

DAY SEVENTY-NINE

Stand firm then, with the belt of truth buckled around your waist, with the breastplate of righteousness in place,
– Ephesians 6:14 NIV

Be wary of the tactics My enemy uses against you. As a defeated foe, the only weapons he wields are lies and deception. To the extent he can penetrate your mind and soul with a lie, he has the ability to insert control. This is quickly brushed aside when you embrace the truth of who I am, what I've done and how I see you now—a dearly-loved child.

Gird yourself with this truth, both in your mind with understanding and in your spirit as testified by My Spirit of Truth. The Holy Spirit will bear witness to what is true, dispelling every lie the enemy foists upon you. Not only is this a protection to you, but for others as well as you speak My truth to those in your world.

One of the most fundamental truths My enemy attacks is the righteous standing you have before Me now through My Son, Jesus. With this truth strapped on as the vitality of your life in Me, it is impenetrable. He attempts to pierce you with shame, condemnation and, in many cases, a belief you must do more to be found worthy in My eyes. Let these fall harmlessly away as you stand in the truth of your righteousness before Me, covered by the blood of My Son, Jesus.

The protection covering you requires faith, for feelings are vulnerable to the attack of the enemy, but your faith is the assurance that secures the victory I have already won. As you walk in Me today, do not fall into a temptation to live out of your feelings, but rather anchor yourself in the fact that what I have said is true.

DAY EIGHTY

[Stand firm then, with the belt of truth buckled around your waist, with the breastplate of righteousness in place,] **and with your feet fitted with the readiness that comes from the gospel of peace.**
– *Ephesians 6:15 NIV*

In the spiritual battle you face, learning how to live in My protection is a critical first step. As you grow in your understanding of what it means to be My warrior, you come to realize that there is more to the battle than holding ground. I am calling you to advance, taking new ground from the enemy. My gospel has power for salvation, not just for you but for those around you that I have called you to take the Good News to.

As you live in the atmosphere of My kingdom—My righteousness, peace and joy—learn that you carry it with you wherever you go. This is significant advancement in the battle, for you are now pushing back the enemy. Always be prepared by living in the power of the gospel with which I am filling you.

To whom can you bring the gospel of peace today? As you live under the showers of My grace, where can you pour out My grace today? As you walk in the freedom of My gospel, learn how My power is working in you to set others free. Be ready, wherever you go each day, to carry the good news of My peace made available to all who ask.

DAY EIGHTY-ONE

In addition to all this, take up the shield of faith, with which you can extinguish all the flaming arrows of the evil one.

– *Ephesians 6:16 NIV*

Your need to understand before you fully trust Me weakens the protection that faith secures. The unspoken need to see with your eyes before you believe in your heart creates vulnerability to attack from the enemy. Beloved, I always do what I say. There is no shadow of turning with Me, for I never change My mind once I have set My will. Believe in the promises I have spoken, trust in the truths that I have proclaimed, and do not wait for understanding or physical evidence to substantiate what is true in the Spirit. Always know that I am working for your best, even if you can't understand or see what I am doing.

When you live in true faith, no matter what the enemy hurls at you, it will not penetrate. Accusation, hatred, doubt, confusion and shame are all extinguished by the shield of faith that surrounds you. And where the enemy has exploited a weakness in your faith, strengthen yourself and return to belief in what is true, and I will remove this stronghold from you. In what ways has your faith been weakened? In what areas are you most susceptible to the enemy's attack? Remember where you have come from, and hold on to what you believe.

DAY EIGHTY-TWO

Take the helmet of salvation and the sword of the Spirit, which is the word of God.
– Ephesians 6:17 NIV

My salvation brings power to renew your mind, the way you think. There are still mental pathways that run unheeded in your mind and flow out of the natural world. Not only is this thinking contrary to My salvation, but it exposes you to great risk of attack from your enemy. Some of these thought patterns have been passed on from previous generations, some are the result of experiences you have had that hurt you; but know this: My salvation, when given full reign in your life, will change the way you think, bringing it into conformity with My truth.

My ways flip the natural world on its head, so it is to your advantage to learn this new perspective on the life I have given you. Not only is it a great safety for you, but it opens the door to advancement in Me, for these new thoughts are founded on the Word of Truth. It is with a renewed mind and the power of My Word that you advance My kingdom on earth.

Having given you what you need, there is much ground I want you to take. This is necessary, for you will either advance or retreat; there is no standing still when it comes to the things of the Spirit. Will you take up My Word today and, with a mind that thinks like Me, step into the possibilities to bring My life and light to the people who are trapped by the devil, just like you were at one time? I am preparing these opportunities for you. Remain alert and aware.

DAY EIGHTY-THREE

And pray in the Spirit on all occasions with all kinds of prayers and requests. With this in mind, be alert and always keep on praying for all the Lord's people. Pray also for me, that whenever I speak, words may be given me so that I will fearlessly make known the mystery of the gospel, for which I am an ambassador in chains. Pray that I may declare it fearlessly, as I should.
– *Ephesians 6:18-20 NIV*

As a soldier in My battle, it is imperative that you never stop praying. Pray in every way you can think of: pray with your mind and understanding, but also pray in the spirit as My Spirit intercedes through you. Pray through song, singing hymns and spiritual songs to Me. Pray in your heart, and pray out loud, declaring the victorious truth of My power at work in this battle you face.

Be aware that a quick prayer, though heard and answered, does not have the sustaining supply you need in this fight. Prayer opens a two-way avenue of communication. Not only are you reaching out to Me with needs and petitions, but you open up a spiritual flow from Me to fill your heart with My assurance, confidence, hope and love. In this way you can fearlessly face the battle in which you contend for My heaven to come into your earth. Practice keeping the avenue of prayer open with Me today. Let your mind turn regularly to the provision that I supply when you open up communication with Me.

DAY EIGHTY-FOUR

Tychicus, the dear brother and faithful servant in the Lord, will tell you everything, so that you also may know how I am and what I am doing. I am sending him to you for this very purpose, that you may know how we are, and that he may encourage you.
– Ephesians 6:21-22 NIV

My child, do not despair or be discouraged in your walk, but open your eyes and see the encouragement I have brought to you. There are people whom I have sent at strategic times to bring companionship, support and words of encouragement. You are not alone, for not only am I your constant companion, but I am giving you people used by Me to build up and strengthen you.

The path of isolation and a heart that guards itself against the exhortation of community will cause your spirit to shrivel and increase the risk of discouragement. Do not lightly set aside the encouraging words of others, for they are sent by Me. They speak words of life, prophetic insight, truth and things I am doing inside of you that lay unseen until spoken out by My servants. Encouragement is a gift I am releasing in your life, but it must be embraced and believed to have full effect. After you have been prepared, release this gift to others for their mutual strengthening. Remember, it is not the quality or quantity of words but My Spirit flowing in this marvelous gift that penetrates a heavy heart.

DAY EIGHTY-FIVE

Peace to the brothers and sisters, and love with faith from God the Father and the Lord Jesus Christ.
– Ephesians 6:23 NIV

Dear child, I speak peace over you today. Why are you so harassed and fearful when I have placed My peace inside of you? Stop; quiet your mind and your heart. I will show you the deep waters of peace that already reside within you by My Spirit. It is the promise of My Son: "My peace I leave with you, My peace I give to you."[a] This peace is established in the knowledge that everything between you and Me has been reconciled.

The conflict you are experiencing in your life is not an indication that you lack My peace, for true peace is not the absence of conflict but the supernatural experience of reconciliation in the midst of tension. There will always be trouble in this world, but it need never touch the deep well of peace I have established within you. On the contrary, My peace is established independent of circumstance.

Therefore, when My peace begins to flow out of you, reconciliation and resolution of conflict begin to bear the fruit of My peace in your world. Acknowledge the fact that some will never choose to accept the peace I offer; but though you feel empathy, their choice is not your responsibility nor should that impact your experience of peace in Me. With your mind quiet and your heart at rest, the still waters of My peace will enhance your ability to experience My love flooding

continued on next page....

your soul and pouring out over your entire being. By faith, receive what I am giving you, and very soon the substantial, yet invisible reality of My peace will begin to impact your visible world.

[a] John 14:27

DAY EIGHTY-SIX

Grace to all who love our Lord Jesus Christ with an undying love.
— Ephesians 6:24 NIV

Precious child, your love moves My heart and fills Me with joy! You do not see Me, yet you love Me; continue to press on seeking My presence. Sometimes you wonder, "Do I love Him enough?" Beloved, every ounce of your voluntary love excites Me, drawing Me close to you. You have responded to My love; in spite of all that stands against you . . . you have chosen love. When you look at Me, I feel overwhelming tenderness and compassion. When you persist, peering through the veil between heaven and earth, seeking Me, loving Me, I am abundantly delighted in you. Though the separation between heaven and earth will continue until My return, you have found the secret of opening heaven's realm . . . your voluntary, extravagantly-loving response to My pursuit.

Today I speak to a fear you have of trial and tribulation. You are concerned your love will grow cold and your faith will be insufficient to face the persecution. Be courageous and unafraid, for when you surrendered your heart to My love, I established within you an undying love for Me. Nothing need diminish your love and the intimacy of our relationship; it is sealed by My Spirit. The things you fear will actually strengthen and deepen your love for Me. This is the joy that is found in hardship, trial and persecution, for in them you are compelled to love

continued on next page....

Me more. So rejoice in Me when these things come, for they are the door to previously-unattainable experiences in My love.

Sit with Me a while longer, expressing your love. In this moment, I am delighted to show you My kingdom more vividly than ever.

TO BE CONTINUED...

ABOUT CF CHURCH

At Christian Fellowship, our mission is to have passion for Jesus Christ and compassion for people. We would love to learn more about you and would like to invite you to join our church family for our Sunday worship service at 10AM!

Children are always welcome in our worship service, but we have a nursery available for infants and toddlers, as well as programs for the children, depending on their age and grade level.

Our worship is lively and contemporary, and we strive to make our teaching for adults applicable and life-giving, according to God's Word. We value authentic relationships and hope that you experience Christ's love through us! Come as you are!

Below are some other ways you can get plugged into our church family:

- **Small Groups**
  - Men's
  - Women's
  - Couples

- **Compassion Ministries**
  - Missions
  - Discovery Groups
  - Prison
  - PADS

- **Youth Ministry**
  - Jr. High
  - Sr. High

- **Children's Ministry**
  - Nursery *(birth to 3yrs)*
  - Primary *(3yrs to 5yrs)*
  - Children's Church *(1st to 5th grade)*

7 VALUES OF CHRISTIAN FELLOWSHIP CHURCH

- Biblical Authority
- Encounter Worship
- Activity of the Holy Spirit
- Authentic Relationships
- Outreach
- Leadership Development
- Kingdom Vision

We hope to see you Sunday. Please feel free to visit our website or call the church office if you have any questions.

CHRISTIAN FELLOWSHIP

3419 Walkup Rd.
Crystal Lake, IL 60012
P: 815.459.9473
E: info@cfchurch.us
www.cfchurch.us

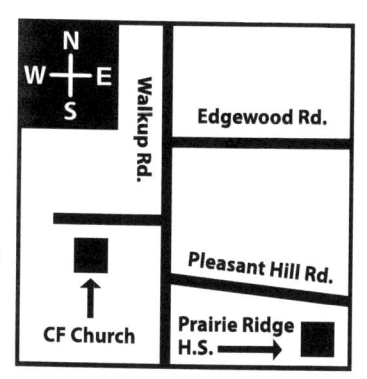

Made in the USA
Lexington, KY
04 April 2017